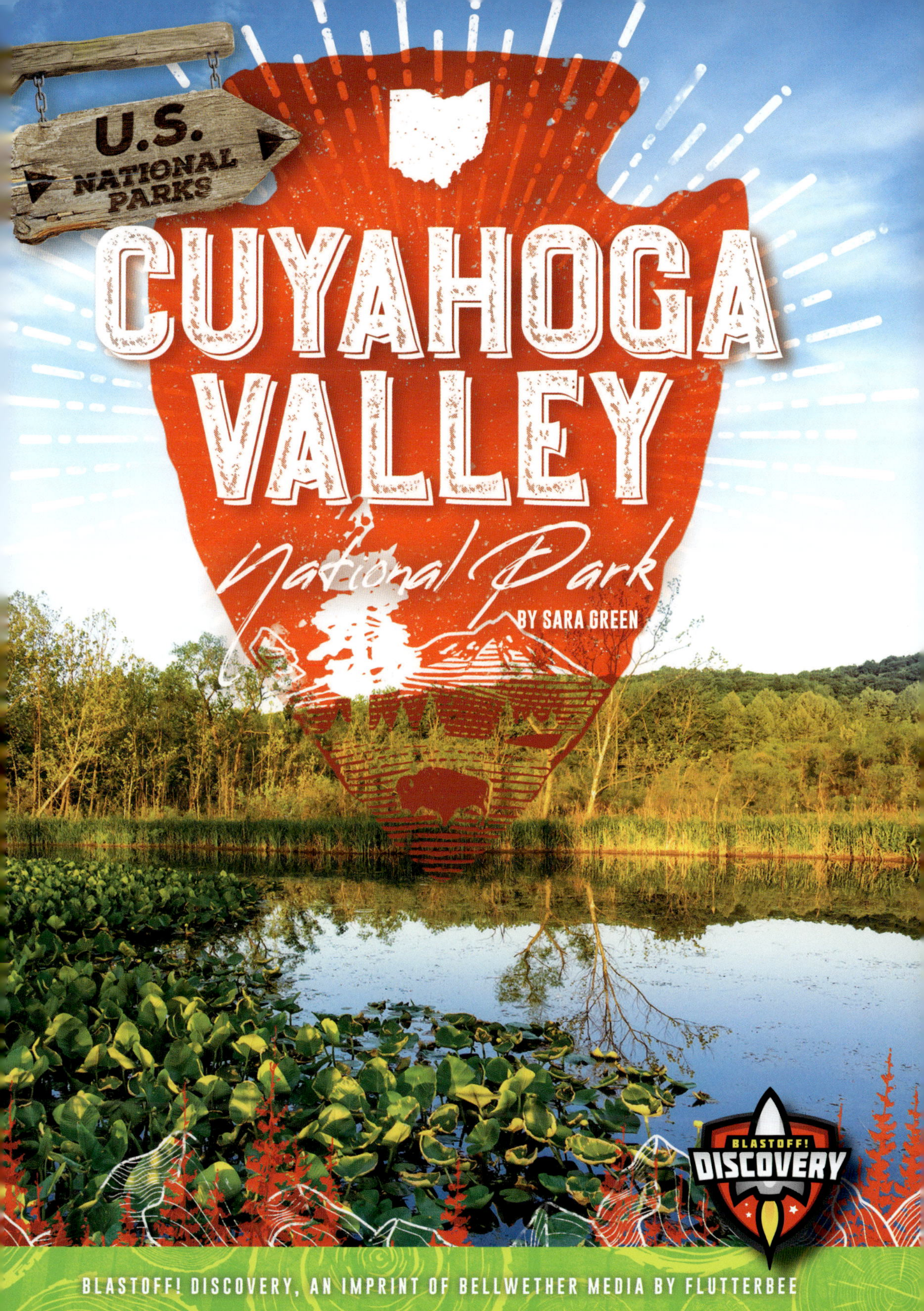

BLASTOFF! DISCOVERY, AN IMPRINT OF BELLWETHER MEDIA BY FLUTTERBEE

This edition first published in 2026 by Bellwether Media, Inc.

Library of Congress Cataloging-in-Publication Data

Names: Green, Sara, 1964- author
Title: Cuyahoga Valley National Park / by Sara Green.
Description: Minneapolis, Minnesota : Bellwether Media, Inc, 2026. | Series: U.S. national parks | Includes bibliographical references and index. | Audience: Ages 8-13 | Summary: "Engaging images accompany information about Cuyahoga Valley National Park. The combination of high-interest subject matter and narrative text is intended for students in grades 3 through 8"–Provided by publisher
Identifiers: LCCN 2025042101 (print) | LCCN 2025042102 (ebook) | ISBN 9798893048476 (hardcover) | ISBN 9798893049473 (ebook)
Subjects: LCSH: Cuyahoga Valley National Park (Ohio)–Juvenile literature
Classification: LCC F497.C95 G74 2026 (print) | LCC F497.C95 (ebook) | DDC 977.1/32–dc23/eng/20250922
LC record available at https://lccn.loc.gov/2025042101
LC ebook record available at https://lccn.loc.gov/2025042102

Editor: Elizabeth Neuenfeldt Designer: Laura Sowers

Printed in the United States of America, North Mankato, MN.

TABLE OF CONTENTS

A PERFECT DAY IN CUYAHOGA VALLEY!

CUYAHOGA VALLEY SCENIC RAILROAD

A family arrives at Cuyahoga Valley National Park. Their first stop is Brandywine Falls. A boardwalk leads them to a scenic viewpoint. It overlooks the towering waterfall! Next, they hike at the Ledges. The trail winds around mossy rocks and past hidden caves. It is magical!

BRIDGE BOOGIE

People are allowed to cross the Everett Covered Bridge on foot, on bikes, or on horses. Some even dance on it. Once a year, people of all ages gather on the bridge for a folk dance!

After lunch, the family hops aboard the historic Cuyahoga Valley Scenic Railroad. The ride offers stunning views of the Cuyahoga River! At day's end, they stop at the Everett Covered Bridge. It has been rebuilt to look like the original bridge from the 1800s. This national park is both beautiful and historic!

CUYAHOGA VALLEY NATIONAL PARK

Cuyahoga Valley National Park lies along the Cuyahoga River in northern Ohio between the cities of Cleveland and Akron. It is one of the country's smallest national parks. It covers 51.5 square miles (133 square kilometers).

Cuyahoga Valley is known for its natural beauty. Trails wind through forests, **wetlands**, and grasslands. Waterfalls cascade along the river. Brandywine Falls, the park's largest waterfall, stands 60 feet (18 meters) tall! The park also has villages, homes, businesses, and a railroad within its boundaries.

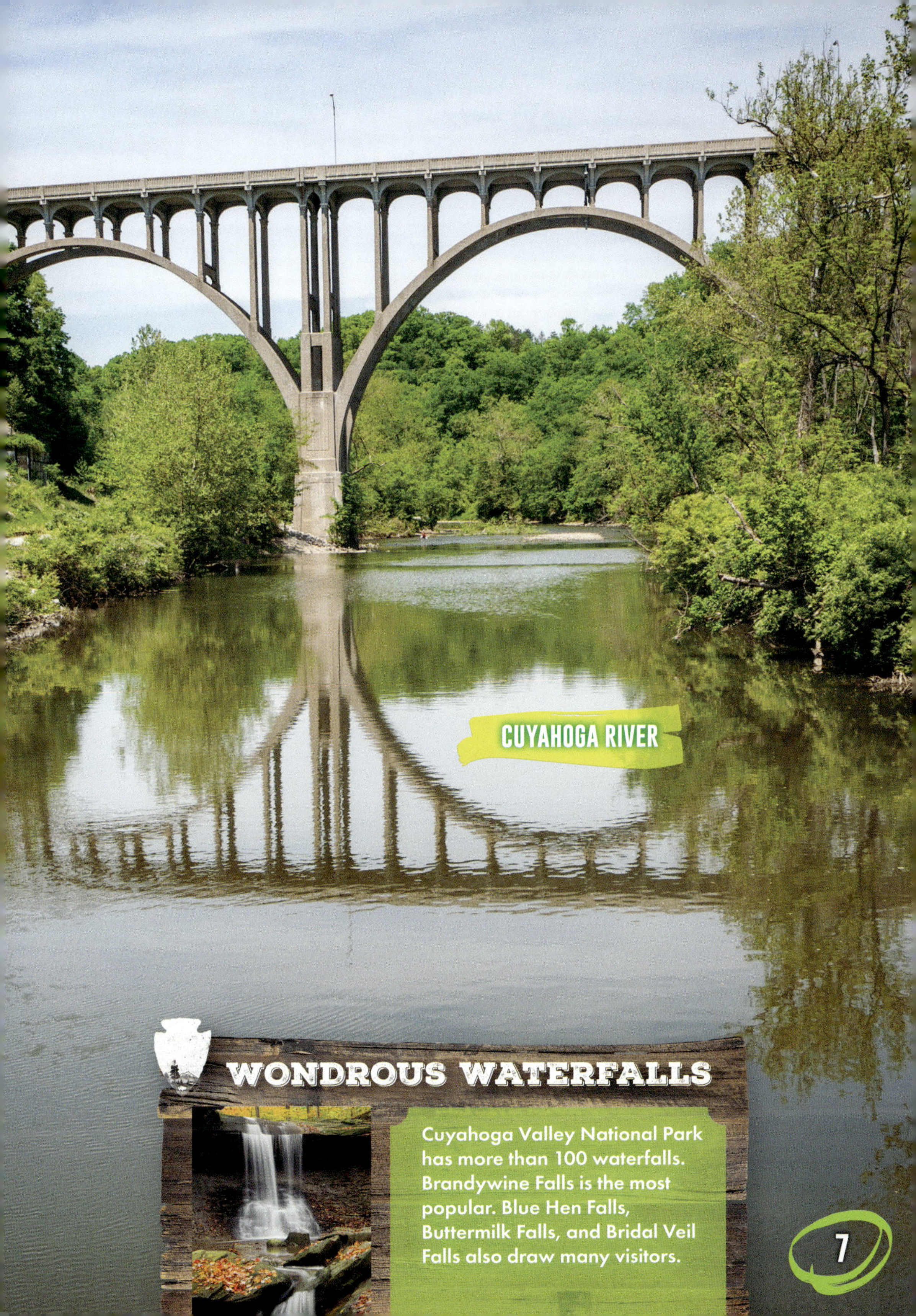

WONDROUS WATERFALLS

Cuyahoga Valley National Park has more than 100 waterfalls. Brandywine Falls is the most popular. Blue Hen Falls, Buttermilk Falls, and Bridal Veil Falls also draw many visitors.

THE LAND

Around 400 million years ago, a sea covered the Cuyahoga Valley. **Sediments** carried in by streams fell to the seafloor. Sediment layers formed and pressed down on one another. **Minerals** in the water glued the layers together and hardened them into rock.

An **ice age** began around two million years ago. **Glaciers** moved across the land and picked up rock, sand, and clay along the way. The glaciers began melting around 10,000 years ago. The rocks, sand, and clay carried by the glaciers were left behind. In time, rivers such as the Cuyahoga River formed and helped create valleys in the area.

HOW SEDIMENTARY ROCKS ARE FORMED

1. Sediments are carried to the sea and fall to the seafloor.

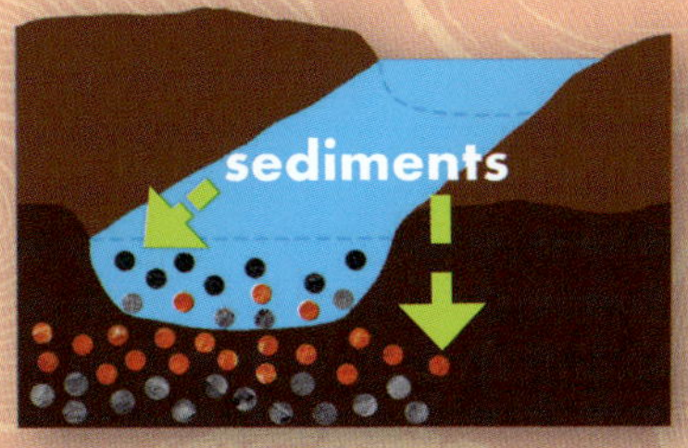

2. Over time, sediment layers form and press down on one another.

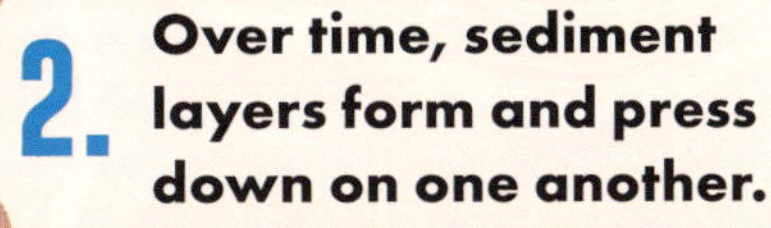
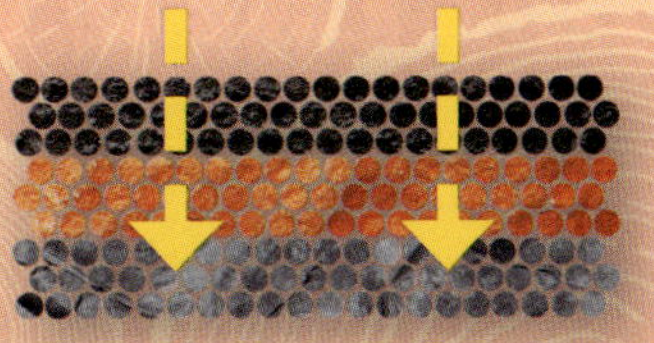

3. Minerals in the water glue the layers together.

4. The layers harden into rock.

Today, the Cuyahoga River winds through the park for about 25 miles (40 kilometers). It provides **habitats** for wildlife in the river and on land. The park has more than 1,500 wetlands. Other natural areas include forests, rolling hills, **ravines**, and waterfalls. Rock formations called the Ledges feature sandstone cliffs, caves, and mossy passageways.

Cuyahoga Valley has four seasons. Summers are warm and **humid**. Winters are cold and snowy. Rain showers are common in spring, while autumn brings cool, crisp days.

PLANTS AND WILDLIFE

Forests cover most of Cuyahoga Valley. **Deciduous** trees such as oak, hickory, and buckeye trees are common. Pine trees also grow in the park. The forests are an important habitat. White-tailed deer nibble on young trees. Gray squirrels and red-bellied woodpeckers nest in taller trees. Foxes, opossums, and cottontail rabbits scurry through the undergrowth. Coyotes hunt nearby.

The park's meadows provide nesting spots for bobolinks, meadowlarks, and other grassland songbirds. Meadow voles snack on big bluestem grass. Monarch butterflies drink nectar from milkweed, goldenrod, and other wildflowers. It gives them the strength to travel to Mexico for winter!

WHITE-TAILED DEER

RED FOX

EASTERN MEADOWLARK

EASTERN COTTONTAIL RABBIT

MEADOW VOLE

One of the largest grassland areas in the park used to be the basketball arena of the Cleveland Cavaliers. After the arena was torn down in 1999, the land was turned back into a natural meadow.

MIGRATORY MONARCH BUTTERFLY

Life Span: up to 9 months
Status: vulnerable

migratory monarch butterfly range =

LEAST CONCERN	NEAR THREATENED	VULNERABLE	ENDANGERED	CRITICALLY ENDANGERED	EXTINCT IN THE WILD	EXTINCT

The park's wetlands provide food and shelter for many types of wildlife. Beavers build dams with mud and sticks. Wood ducks eat duckweed and insects. Great blue herons hunt for fish as painted turtles sun themselves on logs.

GREAT BLUE HERON

TRASH TO TREASURE

The area of the park that is now Beaver Marsh was once a junkyard. People cleaned up the site in the 1980s. Beavers returned and began building dams. Today, Beaver Marsh is a healthy wetland!

More than 65 types of fish live in the park. They include northern pikes and bullheads. River otters play in the water and romp along the shore. Overhead, bald eagles build massive nests in trees near the river.

HUMANS IN CUYAHOGA VALLEY NATIONAL PARK

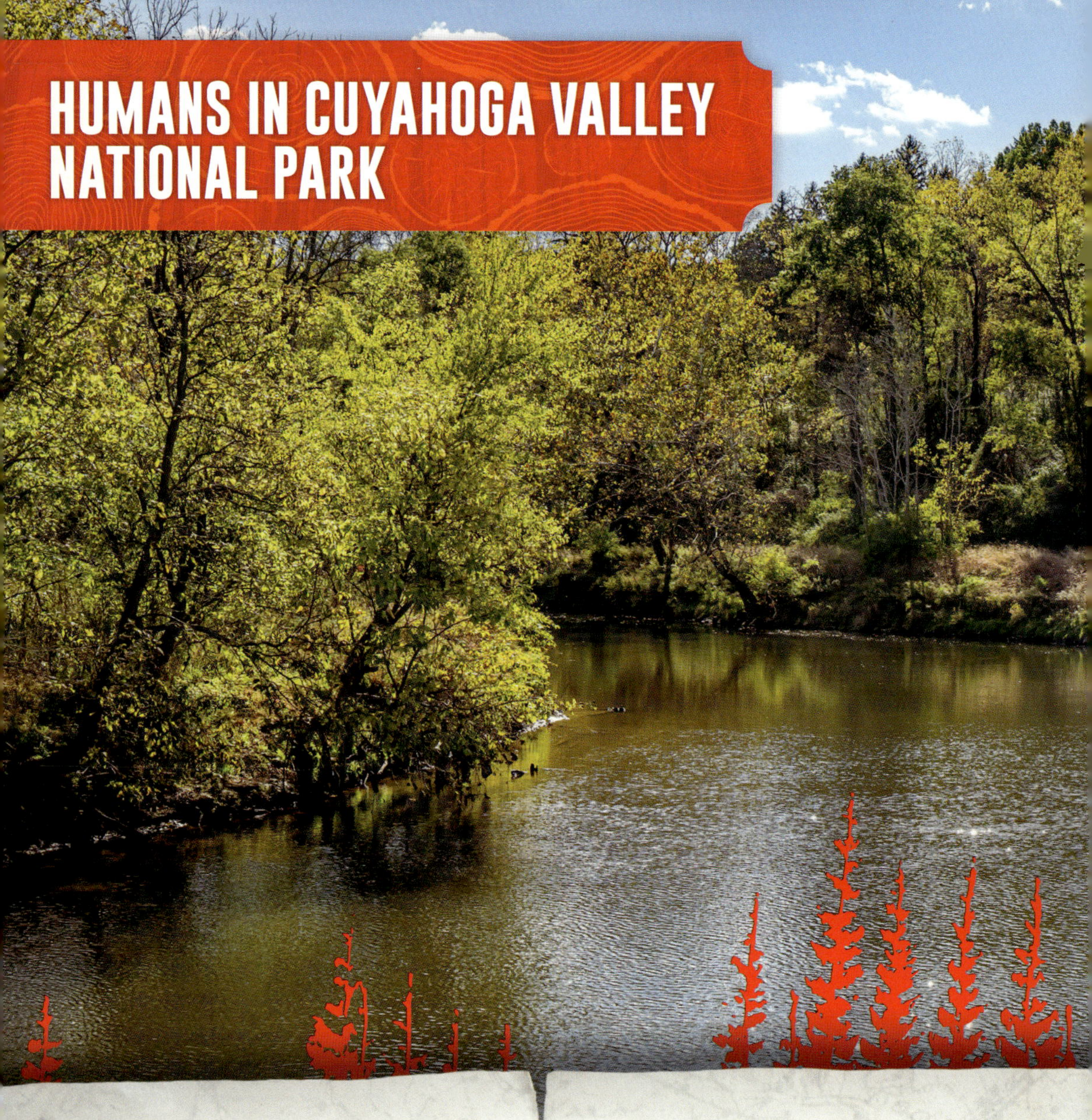

People have been living in the Cuyahoga Valley for more than 12,000 years. Early humans in the valley hunted bison and other large animals. Around 2,000 years ago, the people of the Hopewell **culture** created a large trade network. They traveled on the Cuyahoga River. They made decorative objects from items they traded.

HOPEWELL EARTHWORK

The Hopewell culture is known for its large earthen structures called mounds. The largest mound is believed to have been 500 feet (152 meters) long and 33 feet (10 meters) high.

From around 1000 to 1600, the people of the Whittlesey culture lived in the valley. They grew corn, squash, and beans. They made pottery from the earth and used the land to hunt and gather food.

Europeans made trading posts in the area by the mid-1700s. Around this time, Native American nations such as the Ottawa, Ojibwe, and Seneca lived nearby. But they were forced out around the 1800s.

In 1832, the Ohio & Erie **Canal** was completed. It connected the valley to the Ohio River and Lake Erie. This led to the growth of towns and businesses along the canal. Water pollution grew as people began dumping waste into the Cuyahoga River. By the late 1800s, the river was heavily polluted. Many plants and animals died.

A CANAL BOAT ON THE CUYAHOGA RIVER IN THE 1880s

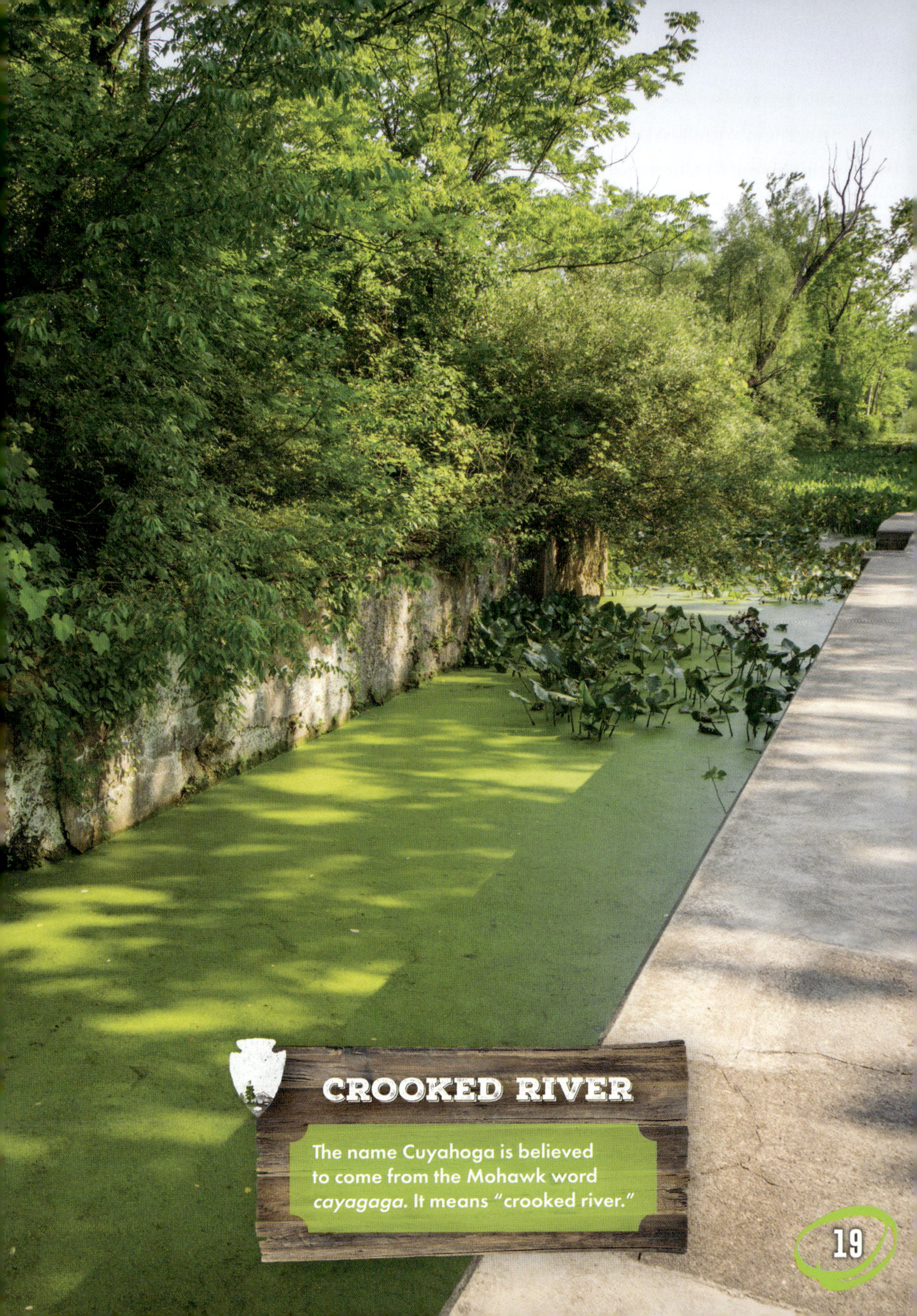

CROOKED RIVER

The name Cuyahoga is believed to come from the Mohawk word *cayagaga*. It means "crooked river."

The Cuyahoga River became more polluted in the 1900s. In 1969, the river caught fire. This made people upset. People began to clean and protect the area. In 1974, President Gerald Ford helped create the Cuyahoga Valley National Recreation Area (CVNRA). This protected the area from more pollution. In the 1980s and 1990s, the park repaired many historic structures.

On October 11, 2000, the CVNRA was renamed Cuyahoga Valley National Park. Park cleanup continued. Local grasses and wildflowers were planted to help create wetlands. Today, the park is a healthy home for wildlife!

A DIRTY DUMP

In 1985, the park bought the former Krejci Dump. People removed over 375,000 tons (340,194 metric tons) of polluted dirt to clean the land!

VISITING CUYAHOGA VALLEY NATIONAL PARK

Cuyahoga Valley National Park offers many activities. Hikers can explore more than 125 miles (201 kilometers) of trails. The Ohio & Erie Canal Towpath Trail allows walking, bicycling, and horseback riding. People enjoy paddling on the Cuyahoga River in kayaks or canoes.

CANAL CENTRAL

The Canal Exploration Center was once a general store and a tavern. Today, it features displays about the Ohio & Erie Canal's history. Visitors can even see a canal lock in action!

TOP SITES

Visitors can peek into the past at the park's historical sites. The Hale Farm & Village features historic buildings, farm animals, and craft demonstrations. People learn about the history of canals and canal boats at the Boston Mill Visitor Center. The Stanford House is a farmhouse built in 1843 that now serves as park lodging.

PROTECTING THE PARK

Cuyahoga Valley's close location to cities makes it easy to visit. It also leads to problems. Air pollution from vehicles and nearby cities can harm plants. Polluted water from cities enters the Cuyahoga River. It can harm people, plants, and animals. Today, the park warns people not to swim in the river.

Invasive species, such as garlic mustard and Japanese knotweed, grow throughout the park. They force out local plants and reduce habitats for songbirds and other wildlife. **Climate change** is another problem. Rising temperatures and heavier rainfall may pose threats to natural areas.

GARLIC MUSTARD

People work hard to protect the park. Park staff and visitors maintain trails. They remove invasive plants and plant local ones along the river to reduce **erosion**. They also replant forests to improve habitats and water quality.

Cuyahoga Valley National Park is part of the National Park Service's Climate Friendly Parks program. Park staff act in many ways to slow climate change. They ride bikes, plant trees, and use less electricity. The park also educates visitors on ways they can manage climate change. Everyone can work together to help protect Cuyahoga Valley National Park!

CUYAHOGA VALLEY NATIONAL PARK FACTS

Area: 51.5 square miles (133 square kilometers)

Area Rank: 55TH largest park

Date Established:
December 27, 1974 (as a national recreation area)
October 11, 2000 (as a national park)

Annual Visitors: 2,912,454 in 2024

Population Rank: 12TH most visited park in 2024

Hiking Trails: more than 125 miles (201 kilometers) of trails

TIMELINE

AROUND 2,000 YEARS AGO

The people of the Hopewell culture live in the Cuyahoga Valley

MID-1700s

Europeans make trading posts in the Cuyahoga Valley

1969

The Cuyahoga River catches fire

FOOD WEB

COYOTE

MEADOW VOLE

WHITE-TAILED DEER

BIG BLUESTEM GRASS

WHITE OAK

1974

President Gerald Ford helps create the Cuyahoga Valley National Recreation Area (CVNRA)

2000

The CVNRA is renamed Cuyahoga Valley National Park

GLOSSARY

canal—a human-made waterway that boats can travel through

climate change—a human-caused change in Earth's weather due to warming temperatures

culture—the beliefs, arts, and ways of life in a place or society

deciduous—related to trees that lose their leaves each year

erosion—the process through which rocks are worn away by wind, water, or ice

glaciers—massive sheets of ice that cover large areas of land

habitats—the natural homes of plants and animals

humid—having a lot of moisture in the air

ice age—a period in Earth's history when the climate was much cooler and large areas of land were covered in sheets of ice

invasive species—plants or animals that are not originally from the area; invasive species often cause harm to their new environments.

minerals—solid, naturally occurring substances

ravines—small, narrow valleys created by running water

sediments—tiny pieces of rocks, minerals, and other natural materials; layers of sediments that are pressed together form sedimentary rocks.

wetlands—areas of land that are covered in low levels of water for much of the year

TO LEARN MORE

AT THE LIBRARY

Payne, Stefanie. *National Parks: Discover All 62 Parks of the United States.* New York, N.Y.: DK Publishing, 2020.

Rathburn, Betsy. *Ohio.* Minneapolis, Minn.: Bellwether Media, 2022.

Woodward, John. *Climate Change.* New York, N.Y.: DK Publishing, 2021.

ON THE WEB

FACTSURFER

Factsurfer.com gives you a safe, fun way to find more information.

1. Go to www.factsurfer.com.
2. Enter "Cuyahoga Valley National Park" into the search box and click 🔍.
3. Select your book cover to see a list of related content.

INDEX

The images in this book are reproduced through the courtesy of: Kenneth Sponsler, front cover, p. 14 (Beaver Marsh); kellyvandellen, pp. 3, 29 (2000); Zack Frank, pp. 4 (railroad), 6-7, 14 (great blue heron), 20 (Frazee House), 23 (Brandywine Falls, Everett Covered Bridge); Patrick Jennings, pp. 4-5; NPS/ Ted Toth/ NPS, p. 5 (bridge); Kenneth Keifer, p. 7; Gestalt Imagery, pp. 8, 28 (mid-1700s); ToddSm66, p. 10; Dee Browning, p. 11; Jim Cumming, p. 12 (eastern cottontail rabbit); rwbrandstetter, p. 12 (white-tailed deer); Marcin Perkowski, p. 12 (red fox); AGAMI, p. 12 (eastern meadowlark); Mike Redmer, p. 12 (meadow vole); Nancy J. Ondra, p. 13; Brian Lasenby, p. 15; Brian Welker/ Alamy Stock Photo, pp. 16-17; Charles O. Cecil/ Alamy Stock Photo, p. 17; NPS Collection/ NPS, p. 18; Zachary Frank/ Alamy Stock Photo, pp. 18-19; David Hume Kennerly/ Wikipedia, p. 20 (Gerald Ford); Daniel, p. 21; NPS/ D.J. Reiser/ NPS, p. 22; NPS/ Bob Trinnes/ NPS, p. 22 (Canal Exploration Center); EWY Media, p. 23 (the Ledges, Cuyahoga Valley Scenic Railroad); Ermell/ Wikipedia, p. 24; Russell Kord/ Alamy Stock Photo, pp. 24-25; NPS/ Victoria Stauffenberg/ NPS, p. 26; Michael Shake, pp. 26-27, 28-29, 30-31, 32; National Park Service/ NPS, p. 28 (around 2,000 years ago); PJ-Stock, p. 28 (1969); Frank John Aleksandrowicz/ Wikipedia, p. 29 (1974); annette shaff, p. 29 (coyote); Stan, p. 29 (meadow vole); ricardoreitmeyer, p. 29 (white-tailed deer); Brian Woolman, p. 29 (big bluestem grass); SHOTPRIME STUDIO, p. 29 (white oak).